ZEBULON PIKE

EXPLORER AND SOLDIER

SPECIAL LIVES IN HISTORY THAT BECOME

Signature LIVES

ZEBULON
PIKE
EXPLORER AND SOLDIER

by Robin S. Doak

Content Adviser: Dr. David Smith,
Adjunct Assistant Professor of History,
University of Michigan

Reading Adviser: Rosemary G. Palmer, Ph.D.,
Department of Literacy, College of Education,
Boise State University

COMPASS POINT BOOKS MINNEAPOLIS, MINNESOTA

Compass Point Books
3109 West 50th Street, #115
Minneapolis, MN 55410

Visit Compass Point Books on the Internet at *www.compasspointbooks.com*
or e-mail your request to *custserv@compasspointbooks.com*

Editor: Editorial Directions
Lead Designer: Jaime Martens
Photo Researcher: Marcie C. Spence
Page Production: The Design Lab, Bobbie Nuytten
Cartographer: XNR Productions, Inc.
Educational Consultant: Diane Smolinski

Managing Editor: Catherine Neitge
Creative Director: Keith Griffin
Editorial Director: Carol Jones

Library of Congress Cataloging-in-Publication Data
Doak, Robin S. (Robin Santos), 1963-
 Zebulon Pike : explorer and soldier / by Robin S. Doak.
   p. cm. -- (Signature lives)
 Includes bibliographical references and index.
 ISBN 0-7565-0998-X (hard cover)
 1. Pike, Zebulon Montgomery, 1779-1813--Juvenile literature. 2.
Explorers--West (U.S.)--Biography--Juvenile literature. 3. Soldiers--United
States--Biography--Juvenile literature. 4. West (U.S.)--Discovery and
exploration--Juvenile literature. 5. Southwest, New--Discovery and explo-
ration--Juvenile literature. 6. Rocky Mountains--Discovery and explo-
ration--Juvenile literature. 7. West (U.S.)--Biography--Juvenile literature.
I. Title. II. Series.
 F592.P653D63 2006
 978'.02'092--dc22   2005002682

Signature Lives

AMERICAN FRONTIER ERA

By the late 1700s, the United States was growing into a nation of homesteaders, politicians, mountain men, and American dreams. Manifest Destiny propelled settlers to push west, conquering and "civilizing" from coast to coast. In keeping with this vision, world leaders hammered out historic agreements such as the Louisiana Purchase, which drastically increased U.S. territory. This ambition often led to bitter conflicts with Native Americans trying to protect their way of life and their traditional lands. Life on the frontier was often filled with danger and difficulties. The people who wove their way into American history overcame these challenges with a courage and conviction that defined an era and shaped a nation.

Table of Contents

1 Chapter

EXPLORING AN UNKNOWN COUNTRY

❦

Under close guard, Zebulon Pike stood defiantly in front of the Spanish general. As a prisoner of Spain, he knew he was treading on dangerous ground. Pike was suspected—with some cause—of being an American spy. And in the 1800s in Mexico and other Spanish territories, the penalty for spying was death. The young Army officer, however, refused to let this scare him.

He had been assigned to explore the western United States, and he intended to finish his job. If Pike could manage to stay alive, he would be able to return to the United States with important information about the Spanish in Mexico.

Although Mexican governor Joaquin del Real Alencaster believed that Pike was spying, he had no real proof. Pike's papers, which Alencaster confiscated, provided no hard evidence of a secret mission. One of the documents the governor examined was General James Wilkinson's written orders to Pike. Wilkinson had instructed Pike to explore the West but also clearly warned him to avoid Spanish territory, for fear of starting a war. They read:

> *It will be necessary you should move with great [carefulness], to keep clear of any Hunting or reconnoitering parties from that province [New Mexico], & to prevent alarm or offence ... it is the desire of the President, to cultivate the Friendship & Harmonious Intercourse, of all the Nations of the Earth, & particularly our near neighbours the Spaniards.*

As a career Army officer, Zebulon Pike lived a life filled with adventure, mystery, and even scandal. He led two difficult and dangerous expeditions into the uncharted regions west of the Mississippi River. On one mission, he became so lost that he wandered into New Spain, Spain's territory in North America. At this time, New Spain included most of what is now the southwestern United States, as well as Mexico and parts of Central and South America. So who, exactly, was Zebulon Pike?

Though several modern-day historians consider him an unsuccessful explorer, Pike was the first

American to investigate the area now known as Kansas, Colorado, and New Mexico. His journeys marked the beginning of America's fascination with life west of the Mississippi. They also set in motion events that would end in the United States' conquest of the Southwest.

Pike's journeys paved the path for future exploration and settlement west of the Mississippi River.

A painting reflects the idea of Manifest Destiny, the belief that Americans were destined to settle the entire North American continent.

Pike's explorations took place in the early 1800s, a time of excitement and uncertainty. The country had only recently earned its independence from Great Britain, growing from 13 separate colonies into the United States of America. The nation was also becoming more crowded. Americans began moving away from the East Coast, pushing farther and farther west. At this time, Americans knew little about what lay in the middle of the vast North American continent. Pike's journals filled in some of the holes in Americans' understanding of this region. The observations of Zebulon Pike would encourage settlers to go west.

The adventures of Pike and others like him would have another long-lasting effect, one that would help shape the size and history of the nation. Not long after Pike's death, Americans began talking about Manifest Destiny, the idea that Americans were destined to settle the North American continent from the Atlantic to the Pacific. Although Zebulon Pike never heard the phrase, he would most certainly have agreed with the concept.

Donald Jackson, a historian who edited Pike's journals, commented, "Nothing that Zebulon Montgomery Pike ever tried to do was easy, and most of his luck was bad." Jackson also published letters, maps, and papers related to Pike and his travels.

2 EARLY LIFE

❧⟨∞⟩❧

Zebulon Montgomery Pike was born in Lamberton, New Jersey, on January 5, 1779. His father, Zebulon Pike, was an officer in the Continental Army. During the Revolutionary War (1775–1783), the elder Pike helped the patriots fight for American independence. He married Zebulon's mother, Isabella Brown of New Jersey, at the start of this conflict.

Young Zebulon was the second oldest of eight children. Four of his siblings, including the first Pike baby, died when they were very young. Zebulon was the oldest surviving child and also the healthiest child in the family. Later in life, siblings James, George, and Maria all suffered from tuberculosis.

At the end of the American Revolution, Zebulon's father moved his family to a farm in Bucks

County, Pennsylvania. Growing up, Zebulon may have attended some local schools, but no records exist. Most of the young man's learning came from his father and, later, from his own studies. Throughout his life, Zebulon would take every opportunity to learn something new. He strongly believed in the importance of education and was an avid reader. As a young Army officer, he even taught himself Latin, French, and Spanish.

Zebulon's father had a strong impact on his son's life. The boy listened eagerly to his tales of action-packed adventure. As a young orphan growing up in colonial New Jersey, Zebulon's father had run away to sea. Later, he became an officer during the Revolutionary War, serving under General George Washington. He continued his career in the military even after the war ended. His stories of battles, bloodshed, and the birth of the United States would fill young Zebulon with dreams of his own.

Zebulon grew up at a time when Americans were packing up and heading west in search of good, cheap land. To help settlers achieve this goal, the U.S. government made deals with some of the native tribes to buy their territory. Other tribes, however, resisted the steadily growing stream of white settlers. As a result, tempers flared and violence between whites and Native Americans was common.

With the country at peace with Great Britain, the

U.S. government turned its attention to the Western frontier. At that time, the United States included everything east of the Mississippi River, except Spanish Florida. A large chunk of land around the Great Lakes called the Northwest Territory was sparsely settled but was growing rapidly. Frontier towns such as Cincinnati, in the Northwest Territory, and Louisville, in Kentucky, needed to be protected from Indian attacks.

Young Zebulon grew up listening to his father's stories about serving under George Washington during the Revolutionary War.

In 1792, Zebulon's father reenlisted with the newly formed U.S. Army to help defend frontier settlements.

The following year, Captain Pike was sent to command Fort Washington, near Cincinnati. Like most other officers, he brought his family with him. Life in a frontier fort was a rough and rugged existence. The Pikes lived in a small fortress with about 150 other soldiers. The fort was surrounded by high log walls to keep the Indians out.

In 1794, 15-year-old Zebulon joined his father's company as a cadet, a young man training to be an officer. Zebulon's first job in the Army was to take supplies from Fort Washington to other frontier posts along the Miami River. Carrying food and other items, he traveled the river by barge and then on foot along forest pathways. His route took him as far as Fort Detroit (present-day Detroit, Michigan), a

In 1794, Zebulon went with his family to live at Fort Washington. During this time, he joined his father's troop and trained as an officer.

distance of more than 250 miles (402 kilometers). In the coming years, Zebulon would follow his father and his regiment to other forts on the Western frontier.

In March 1799, Zebulon received orders to take command as a second lieutenant. He was a responsible, disciplined officer, and within eight months he was promoted to first lieutenant. Zebulon spent his first few years as an officer in posts along the Western frontier. One of his early assignments was in western Pennsylvania, where he had spent part of his boyhood.

While living in Indiana and Illinois in 1803, Pike wrote frequently to his family. He liked to give advice to his sister, Maria, who was 13 at the time. One letter advised her to "employ what leisure time you can command in reading and writing. Your words are generally well spelt, but the writing is bad. Practice more and learn to write without quite so much flourish."

As an officer, 1st Lieutenant Zebulon Pike enjoyed sporting activities. He was an expert shot with the rifle. Physically, he was fairly ordinary. He stood about 5 feet 8 inches (173 centimeters) tall and had light hair and blue eyes. His personality was much more remarkable, however. Pike's fellow soldiers knew him as a highly honorable and very patriotic officer. The young man took his duties seriously, and he expected other soldiers to do the same.

Pike never drank alcohol, and he sometimes seemed too strict. One tale related how he would

vi   C O N T E N T S.

T H E

FEDERALIST:

ADDRESSED TO THE

PEOPLE OF THE STATE OF
NEW-YORK.

NUMBER I.

Introduction.

AFTER an unequivocal experience of the ineffi-
cacy of the fubfifting federal government, you
are called upon to deliberate on a new conftitution for
the United States of America. The fubject fpeaks its
own importance; comprehending in its confequences,
nothing lefs than the exiftence of the UNION, the
fafety and welfare of the parts of which it is com-
pofed, the fate of an empire, in many refpects, the
moft interefting in the world. It has been frequently
remarked, that it feems to have been referved to the
people of this country, by their conduct and example,
to decide the important queftion, whether focieties of
men are really capable or not, of eftablifhing good
government from reflection and choice, or whether
they are forever deftined to depend, for their political
conftitutions, on accident and force. If there be any
truth in the remark, the crifis, at which we are arrived,
may with propriety be regarded as the æra in which
                          A   that

Documents published by the Federalists, a political party that Pike strongly supported

hide in the bushes in order to catch his men drinking
and causing a disturbance. If Pike caught one of his
soldiers acting improperly, he would immediately
have him punished.

Pike also followed politics. He was a supporter
of the Federalists, a political party that favored a
strong central government and a large Army and
Navy, even during peacetime. In June 1799, Pike
took part in the public whipping of a newspaper editor who openly opposed Federalist policies.

In the early 1800s, Pike fell in love with his intel-
ligent young cousin, Clarissa Brown of Kentucky.
Pike affectionately called her Clara. Although

Clara's father, Pike's uncle, refused to give his permission to marry, Pike persisted. In 1801, he and 18-year-old Clara eloped to Cincinnati. Brown didn't want his daughter to have to endure the rough and sometimes dangerous life of an Army wife. After Clara's marriage, Brown refused to see or speak to the pair, and he and his daughter never completely reconciled.

In 1802, Pike was transferred to a new infantry unit, and the newlyweds moved to Fort Knox. The fort was located near Vincennes, Kentucky, in the Indiana Territory, which was formed in 1800 from part of the Northwest Territory. The new Indiana Territory included present-day Wisconsin, Illinois, and Indiana, as well as half of what is now Michigan. Although Vincennes was the capital of the Indiana Territory, it was little more than a tiny frontier town. The only buildings in the capital were a schoolhouse, sawmill, and tavern.

The Pikes' only surviving daughter married John C. S. Harrison, the son of U.S. President William Henry Harrison. The couple had six children, including a son named Montgomery Pike and a daughter named Zebuline.

Clara had difficulty adjusting to her new life as the wife of an Army officer. Cut off from her family, she now found herself living in a dirty, uncomfortable fort surrounded by soldiers. There was little to do but play cards with other officers' wives, dance, garden, and gossip.

In 1803, Pike was transferred to a post in Kaskaskia, Illinois. Clara went with her husband, but the change in scenery did not improve her outlook. In a letter to his mother, Pike wrote, "Clara is at present very nervous and her situation here is very lonesome as the ladies are by no means sociable." He wrote to his sister, Maria, that his wife should "cheer up and try to be lively."

Pike himself found life in Illinois difficult. He got measles soon after arriving and was so sick that he could not perform his duties for several weeks. The one bright spot in the young family's existence was the birth of daughter Clarissa on February 24, 1803. Clarissa was the only one of five Pike children to survive childhood.

A military fort in Illinois, in the early 1800s

Despite the disapproval of Clara's family, the

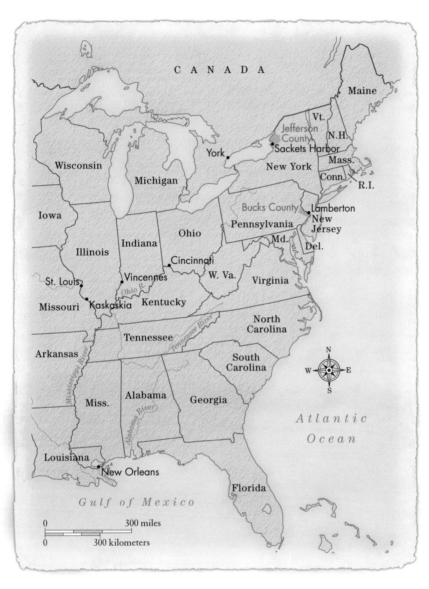

Pikes' marriage lasted through long separations, public scandal, and the death of several children. After Pike's early death in 1813, Clara wore black for the rest of her life. ✒

As an Army officer, Pike lived in various forts east of the Mississippi.

3 A CHANCE FOR ADVENTURE

※

The year 1803 was a momentous one for Americans. On April 3, President Thomas Jefferson purchased a huge area of land west of the Mississippi River from France. With one stroke of a pen—and $15 million— Jefferson doubled the size of the United States. The sale made Americans the proud owners of nearly 828,000 square miles (2,152,800 square kilometers) of land between the Mississippi River and the Rocky Mountains.

The purchase immediately created problems between the United States and Spain. The Louisiana Territory had, until recently, been controlled by the Spanish. In need of money, Spain had secretly made a deal to sell the region to France in October 1800. One condition of the sale was that France had to

President Thomas Jefferson doubled the size of the United States by purchasing land west of the Mississippi River.

promise to keep the land and not sell it. The Spanish did not want their westward-moving neighbors, the Americans, coming any closer to New Spain. So when Spain's leaders learned that France had violated their agreement and sold the land to the United States, they were furious. They refused to recognize the Louisiana Purchase.

Spain and the United States also disagreed on the exact boundaries of the Louisiana Territory. The southern and western boundaries in particular had not been specified in the treaty between the United States and France. When the U.S. minister to France, Robert Livingston, asked the French foreign minister Charles-Maurice de Talleyrand-Périgord to clarify the boundaries, he refused to do so. He told Livingston, "You have made a noble bargain for yourselves and I suppose you will make the most of it."

As a result, the Americans claimed all of the land from the Mississippi River to the sources of its major tributaries, including the Missouri River in the north and the Arkansas and Red rivers in the south. The Spanish more narrowly defined the sale, saying that the territory did not include

All or part of 15 U.S. states were later created from land that was part of the Louisiana Purchase: Arkansas, Colorado, Iowa, Kansas, Louisiana, Minnesota, Missouri, Montana, Nebraska, New Mexico, North Dakota, Oklahoma, South Dakota, Texas, and Wyoming.

Robert Livingston, the U.S. minister to France, negotiated the Louisiana Purchase.

any part of the Great Plains or the Rocky Mountains. It seemed that only a war between the two nations would put an end to the dispute.

One of President Jefferson's top priorities was to learn more about his new purchase. To accomplish this goal, he sent Army officers Meriwether Lewis and William Clark on an expedition to explore, map, and document the land. Jefferson wanted the two to keep careful notes on the geography, plants, animals, and people of the region. On Lewis' way to St. Louis, Missouri, he passed through Kaskaskia, and Pike almost certainly met him. In fact, a number of men in Pike's regiment signed up with Lewis to be part of the adventure.

In June 1805, Pike was ordered to report to St. Louis. Although he was now the commander of Fort Kaskaskia, the young officer was thrilled to receive new orders. Until then, his time in the Army had been rather boring. With no wars raging, Pike had no chance to do anything really remarkable or to distinguish himself with acts of heroism or bravery. But his hard work and devotion to duty had attracted the attention of his superiors.

One man who had taken an interest in the hardworking first lieutenant was General James Wilkinson. A friend of President Jefferson, Wilkinson had acted as the U.S. representative when the Louisiana Territory was officially transferred from France to the United States in the winter of 1803. In December, Wilkinson and another American traveled to New Orleans for the transfer ceremony. Here, the French commissioner handed the U.S. officials the keys to the city. This gesture symbolized the beginning of American control in the region. In 1805, the president made Wilkinson governor of the Louisiana Territory. He also served as the commander of all U.S. military forces.

Wilkinson, however, was not who he presented himself to be. Since 1787, the general had officially worked as a secret agent for the Spanish. Known in Spain as Agent 13, Wilkinson was paid $2,000 a year to supply the Spanish with military secrets. At the same time, he was also passing Spanish documents to the United States. The information Wilkinson passed from one country to another was often completely false, made up by the general in order to achieve his own personal goals.

General James Wilkinson was governor of the Louisiana Territory.

Some historians believe that Wilkinson hoped to conquer parts of the Southwest and found an empire with Vice President Aaron Burr. Many believe that Wilkinson and Burr wanted to provoke Spain and the United States into war. That way, the general would have an excuse to send his troops into Spain's southwestern territories and take control.

Pike, however, probably knew nothing of Wilkinson's plans. To him, Wilkinson was a friend and role model, the person who was giving him his big chance for adventure. Pike arrived in St. Louis, the capital of the Louisiana Territory, in late July 1805. The town, which had become part of the United States after the Louisiana Purchase, would serve as a gateway to the West for explorers and settlers alike. Established as a French trading post in 1764, St. Louis grew quickly as people from the East headed there, looking for guides to lead them safely into the wild new lands.

In his book Winning the West, *Theodore Roosevelt offered this description of James Wilkinson: "He was a good-looking, plausible, energetic man, gifted with a taste for adventure ... He had no conscience and no scruples; and he had not the slightest idea of the meaning of the word honor ... He was treacherous to the Union while it was being formed and after it was formed."*

When Pike arrived in St. Louis, he reported to Wilkinson to receive his orders. The general told Pike he would be commanding a mission of exploration. Pike was to take a party of soldiers up the Mississippi River in search of the river's source. Along the way, he would have other missions to accomplish. Wilkinson wanted Pike to meet with and observe the native tribes he came across while traveling. Pike was to encourage warring tribes in the region to make peace with one another. He was also to buy

St. Louis became known as a gateway to the West.

areas of land on which the Army could later build forts. In addition, he was told to collect scientific and astronomical data.

To avoid the winter weather, Pike was instructed to leave St. Louis in early August. This left him little time to prepare. Before leaving, Pike had to select the men to go with him and gather the supplies they would need. He also had to learn as much as possible about his route before he set off.

Because of the hasty arrangements, Pike was unable to find a physician or a translator to travel with him. And he was provided with few scientific instruments for collecting the desired data. The items he did have were very basic. They included a watch, a thermometer, and a theodolite, which is an

Even though Pike and his men had few supplies, they were excited to begin their journey along the Mississippi.

instrument used by surveyors to measure angles and directions. When describing the first journey, Pike would later write that he had "no gentleman to aid me, and I literally performed the duties (as far as my limited abilities permitted) of astronomer, surveyor, commanding officer, clerk, spy, guide, and hunter."

Pike packed enough food and supplies to last for four months in the wilderness. He and his men carried flour, whiskey, cornmeal, pork, gunpowder, salt, and tobacco. Other supplies included tents, blankets, writing paper, ink, flags, and hunting dogs. Pike and his men also brought items that could be given to the Indians as gifts, including calico cloth and knives. Despite the lack of time to prepare, Pike was excited about the journey. He had full trust in his own abilities and believed that this was his chance to prove his worth. ஒ

4 THE FIRST EXPEDITION

☙✦❧

On August 9, 1805, 26-year-old Zebulon Pike and 20 men set off from Fort Bellefontaine in St. Louis. The men began their journey on a keelboat, a shallow, flat-bottomed boat used on rivers to cart supplies from one place to another.

Much of Pike's trip involved visiting the villages of the native tribes in the region. Along the way, he met the Sauk, Fox, Sioux, and Chippewa. As he traveled, the lieutenant observed tribal customs, ate native foods, and listened to folk tales and legends. Pike would later publish accounts of these visits.

The men followed a general routine during the expedition. They rose at sunup and traveled for two hours before stopping to eat breakfast. Then they continued on until the early afternoon, when they

Pike and his men encountered several Indian tribes, including Sauk and Fox, on their first expedition.

stopped and prepared lunch. The explorers set up camp for the night around 6 P.M. After putting up their tents, they lit a large fire to cook supper and keep warm. After supper, they might have passed the time by talking or playing cards.

Pike spent his evenings carefully recording his thoughts in his journal. He also used the quiet nights to catch up on his reading and to advance his learning.

On this and a later trip, Pike carried a number of books with him. After hiking several miles during the day, he read about battle tactics, warfare, and other subjects in the flickering light of a bonfire.

By September 4, Pike and his men reached Prairie du Chien, a village and trading post located at the spot where the Wisconsin River empties into the Mississippi. But the keelboat that the party had been using was too big to portage, or carry, around the waterfalls and rapids that were ahead. So the party left the boat behind and switched to four smaller, lighter vessels.

On September 23, Pike and his men met with members of the Dakota Sioux tribe at the junction of the Mississippi and Minnesota rivers. Here, Pike purchased more than 155,000 acres (62,725 hectares) of land from the tribe. In exchange for the land, he gave the Sioux $200 worth of presents and 60 gallons (227 liters) of whiskey. He also promised that the U.S. government would pay the tribe $2,000 at a later date.

Pike left the Sioux and went on to the Falls of St. Anthony in present-day Minneapolis, Minnesota. Here, he and his men pushed, pulled, and carried

Some members of Pike's party spent a lot of time hunting. That's because every day, each man ate between 7 and 8 pounds (3 and 4 kilograms) of meat to survive. Extra meat was usually preserved in salt. Later, it was boiled in a pot with flour, wild rice, or corn to make soup.

their boats and supplies around the waterfall. They then continued to paddle their way up the Mississippi River in search of its source.

By early October, winter weather began to set in. The challenging trip now became even more difficult. The men trekked through snow, freezing rain, and raw winds. Several of Pike's men became ill. Pike wrote, "My Sergeant one of the Stoutest men I ever knew, broke a blood-vessel and vomited nearly two quarts of blood." Those who became too sick or tired to paddle the boats were forced to follow along by foot on the river bank or be left behind.

On October 15, Pike realized that his men were near their breaking point. He wrote, "[Even] if I had no regard for my own health and constitution, I should have some for these poor fellows, who were killing themselves to obey my orders." Just below Little Falls in Minnesota, Pike and the others built a basic fort and decided to stay for a while. Here, they began constructing new pine canoes they hoped would carry them to the source of the Mississippi. Although Pike didn't know it, his mission was less than half over. It would be another six months before he and his men returned to St. Louis.

Nearly two months later, Pike finally felt ready to begin the final part of his mission. On December 10, the party set out to find the Mississippi's source. Because the river had frozen, Pike and his men

pulled the canoes, along with two large sleds, behind them. They dragged the supplies over rocks and snow on the prairies. When Pike thought the river ice was thick enough, he had the men pull the sleds over the ice. Less than a week after setting out, however, one of the big sleds fell through the ice and was lost. Pike's books and baggage, as well as gunpowder and rifle cartridges, were damaged.

Pike and his men were determined to find the source of the Mississippi River. As they traveled, they encountered several Indian villages.

The group's bad luck persisted. In early January, Pike's tents caught on fire, and his socks, leggings,

Pike and his crew faced a bitter winter and the frozen waters of the Mississippi.

and moccasins were burned. The bitter winter weather also continued, causing some of the men to get frostbite. Pike wrote, "The cold was so intense, that some froze their noses—some their fingers and some their toes." Traveling was extremely difficult.

But on January 8, 1806, Pike's luck began to change. He and his men came across a British trading post. Inside, the men were treated to a warm meal, dry clothes, and a roaring fire. Nearly two weeks later, Pike set off for Leech Lake, believed at that time to be the source of the Mississippi. It was located about 30 miles (48 km) west of present-day Grand Rapids, Minnesota. Only one of Pike's men accompanied him on this journey. The rest were too ill to continue.

On February 1, Pike reached the lake. He believed—mistakenly—that he had found the source of the Mississippi River. "I will not attempt to describe my feelings on the accomplishment of my voyage," he wrote in his journal.

During their trip, Pike and his men were spectators at a ball game between the Sioux and the Fox and Winnebago tribes. The game, similar to lacrosse, used a hard leather ball and 3-foot (1-meter) sticks with a net attached to one end. Pike wrote, "He who drives the ball round the Goal, is much shouted by his companions." The match went on for four hours before the Sioux won.

Thinking his mission was a success, Pike turned around and headed home. He and his men finally reached St. Louis on April 30, 1806. By this time, they had traveled more than 5,000 miles (8,047 km) and spent nearly nine months in the wilderness.

Today, most historians agree that Pike's trip was not much of a success. Contrary to his own belief, Pike had not found the source of the Mississippi. Not until 1832 would geographer Henry Schoolcraft locate the lake in Minnesota where the river actually begins. Schoolcraft called the lake Itasca, a name he coined from the Latin phrase *veritas caput*, or "true source." From Itasca,

During his nine-month journey, Pike was able to gather important information about the land and people of the upper Mississippi.

the Mississippi flows north and then east before curving southward and cutting a long pathway through the heart of North America.

Despite his failure to find the Mississippi's source, Pike did accomplish several of his goals. He secured a peace treaty with the Sioux and gathered valuable information about the people and geography of the upper Mississippi. Pike also made maps of the places he and his men had traveled. Although these maps were not well drawn and he had discovered nothing new, his writings and drawings would ultimately attract people to settle in the upper Mississippi region.

More importantly, Pike's first journey helped prepare him for his next trip, an expedition that would be far more difficult and dangerous. Pike had learned that he could lead his men safely into the wilderness and back again—without accurate maps or dependable scientific equipment. When the time came, Pike would be ready and eager to once again explore America's wild frontier. ❧

5 INTO DANGEROUS TERITORY

❦

Upon their return to St. Louis, Pike and his men were exhausted and ready for a much-deserved rest. But General Wilkinson had other plans. Soon after Pike arrived home, the general gave him a new mission. This time, Pike was ordered to explore the western mountains "approximate to the settlements of New Mexico." Further, he was to locate the source of the Arkansas and Red rivers, then travel down the Red.

Pike knew that this mission had the potential to be dangerous. At that time, the rivers served as part of the boundary between the United States and Spanish Mexico. If Pike and his men strayed into Spanish territory, they ran the risk of being arrested for spying. And the young officer knew the penalty

The capital of New Spain was Mexico City. If Pike had ventured into Spanish territory, his life would have been in danger.

for spying in New Spain—death. He would also have to leave his wife Clara, his daughter Clarissa, and an infant son behind at Fort Bellefontaine. Despite his concerns, Pike viewed the assignment as another opportunity to prove his worth to his country.

Pike had another set of orders, as well. Wilkinson wanted the lieutenant to spy on the Spanish in New Spain. At that time, the relationship between the United States and Spain was falling apart. Both countries still argued about the boundaries of the Louisiana Purchase, and President Jefferson had recently ordered more troops to defend Fort Claiborne in present-day Louisiana. Pike was probably convinced he was doing his patriotic duty by gathering information against a possible enemy.

Pike was correct in guessing that any information he collected would be useful to the United States. What he likely didn't know was how useful this knowledge of the Southwest would be to James Wilkinson and Aaron Burr. If the two were actually going to send troops to invade the region, they needed as many facts as possible about the land west of the Mississippi. They especially needed to learn about how well New Spain was defended: How many troops did the Spanish have near the U.S. border? What types of fortresses had they built to defend their land?

Most historians believe Pike was not involved in

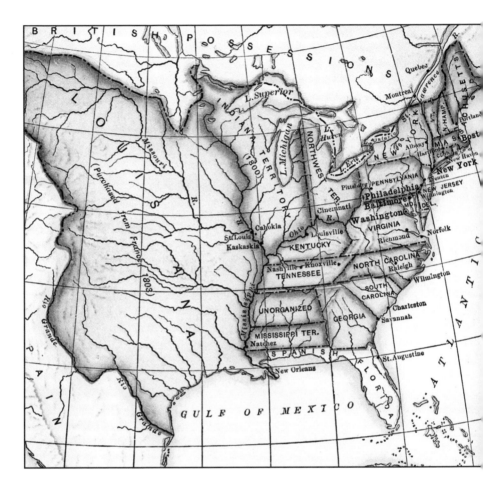

The United States after the Louisiana Purchase

the treasonous plan that Wilkinson and Burr had hatched. It is known, however, that President Jefferson did not authorize Pike's second mission—though he approved once he learned of it.

On July 15, 1806, Pike and 22 men set off from Fort Bellefontaine. Seventeen of the men were soldiers who had been with Pike on his first expedition. Two volunteer soldiers had also signed on for the adventure, and Wilkinson's son, Lieutenant James Biddle Wilkinson, was there as Pike's second in command.

Only two of the men in the party were not soldiers. One, John Hamilton Robinson, was a young surgeon who had been hired by a local merchant to collect a $2,000 debt in Santa Fe, the capital of Spain's New Mexico territory. Some historians believe that Dr. Robinson had also been hired by General Wilkinson to spy on the Spanish. The other nonmilitary man was A. F. Baronet Vasquez, a native trapper who would serve as a translator. Pike was quite pleased with his group, which he affectionately called a "set of rascals."

Unfortunately, the party was headed for trouble. Once again, the group was ill-prepared for the trip. The men did not take any winter clothes because Pike didn't believe they would come across any cold weather. Pike still lacked much scientific equipment, although this time he did have a telescope. Finally, the only chart Pike had to guide him through the region was an inaccurate map made by German scientist Alexander Von Humboldt. This brilliant scientist had worked on the map for the Spanish in the early 1800s. He called his chart the General Map for the Kingdom of New Spain. But Humboldt had not visited the areas he had mapped. Instead, he relied on knowledge that he had collected from

Scientist and mapmaker Alexander Von Humboldt

trappers, traders, and natives in the region.

Pike and his men began their journey by heading west on the Missouri River. Their first stop was an Osage village on the Osage River near the current border of Kansas and Missouri. There, Pike returned about 50 Osage and Pawnee Indians who had been held captive by another tribe. On their way home, the Indians had followed Pike on land as he and his men sailed along the river.

Part of Pike's mission was to ease relations between American settlers and the native people of the West. Pike's task was to convince the Indians that they were better off under U.S. control than under Spanish, French, or British rule. The return of the native captives was meant to help accomplish this mission. It seemed to work. After the newly freed captives arrived home, one of the Osage chiefs made the following speech:

On the second trip, Pike's men braved drenching rainstorms, rough terrain, and wild animals. Pike described one close scrape with a rattlesnake: "Today in our tour I passed over a remarkably large rattlesnake as he lay curled up, and trod so near him as to touch him with my foot ... I then turned around and touched him with my ram-rod, but he showed no disposition to bite, and appeared quite [peaceful]. The gratitude which I felt towards him for not having bit me induced me to save his life."

> *Osage, you now see your wives, your brothers, your daughters, your sons redeemed from captivity. Who did this? Was it the Spanish? No! The French? No! Had either of those people been governors of the country your relatives might have rotted in captivity, and you never would have seen them, but the Americans stretched forth their hands, and they are returned to you!*

While he was staying with the Osage, Pike received a message from his wife, Clara. The letter noted that Pike's children had been ill. Pike could only pray for the best. Until his journey was completed, he could not return to his family. Pike's little son died a month later, a fact that Pike would not learn until he returned from his trip.

In early September 1806, Pike's party left the Osage village and headed west across the Kansas plains. The men were astounded by the huge herds of buffalo, antelope, and deer. But Pike was discouraged by the large stretches of desertlike land. He later described the region as a "great wasteland"

During their travels across the Kansas plains, Pike's party saw herds of buffalo.

that was "incapable of cultivation." In the published account of his journey, he wrote, "These vast plains of the western hemisphere may become in time equally celebrated as the sandy deserts of Africa." Pike's opinion would be seconded by Army officer Stephen Harriman Long, who explored the Rocky Mountains from 1818 to 1823. Their statements gave rise to the myth of the Great American Desert, a huge arid area in the center of North America.

Pike did believe that the Plains could serve one useful purpose: keeping Americans from settling beyond the Mississippi. "Our citizens being so prone to rambling and extending themselves," he wrote, "will, through necessity, be constrained to limit their extent on the West, to the borders of the Missouri and Mississippi, while they leave the prairies ... to the wandering and uncivilized Aborigines [Indians] of the country."

Pike was wary of the "wandering and uncivilized" natives that he met on his trip. One day, while crossing the Great Plains, Pike's party was

The idea of the Great American Desert would quickly prove false. In 1837, American inventor John Deere built a special plow with steel-tipped prongs. The plow could easily break through the hard soil of the Great Plains. By 1842, Deere had begun selling his plows in Illinois. Farming soon became important in the region. Today, the Great Plains states are a major farming area.

approached by a Pawnee hunting party. The Indians outnumbered the soldiers two to one. The Pawnee seemed friendly but soon became upset when they thought that Pike was not giving them enough presents. Before long, they began to take the supplies and equipment that Pike and his men needed to complete their trip. Pike ended the conflict by promising to shoot the next Indian who tried to steal from him. The Pawnee left peacefully. ❧

Pike and his men had a run-in with a Pawnee hunting party while crossing the Great Plains.

6 HUNTED MEN

After crossing the Plains, Pike came to a Pawnee village on the Republican River, near the border of present-day Kansas and Nebraska. The Pawnee were flying the Spanish flag. The Spanish, who had been exploring the Southwest since the 1500s, had a long history of communication with the native people in the region. In addition, Spanish troops under the command of Facundo Melgares had just left the village.

Melgares was looking for Pike and his men. From the moment the party left St. Louis, the Spanish knew that the Americans were coming. Since then, they had been waiting and watching for Pike. How did the Spanish know of Pike's expedition? General James Wilkinson had notified the

Francisco Vásquez de Coronado (second from left) was one of several Spanish explorers who journeyed through the Southwest during the 1500s.

Spanish government that Pike was on his way. No one knows for certain why Wilkinson did this.

Upon arriving in the Pawnee village, Pike immediately demanded that the Spanish flag be taken down. He told the Pawnee that "it was impossible for the nation to have two fathers; that they must either be the children of the Spaniards or acknowledge their American father." Pike's speech appeared to work. The Native Americans took down the Spanish flag and raised the Stars and Stripes.

Afterward, however, the Pawnee seemed hostile and unwilling to let Pike continue on his way. The lieutenant firmly insisted they were leaving. Later, the Native Americans chief described the scene to an Indian agent, who retold the story:

> *The morning came, and the rising sun found Pike with his men, all mounted, well armed and equipped; their heavy broadswords drawn. The old Warrior Chief had summoned his forces also, and there they stood, more than Five hundred in number, armed with Bows and Arrows, spears and tomahawks, in gloomy silence; each party waiting in painful suspense the orders of their respective chiefs. The chief recalled that he approached Pike and earnestly urged him to cancel his journey. Pike pointed to a spot in the sky just above the eastern horizon, and told the chief he would set*

out when the sun reached that spot, saying that 'nothing but death can stop us— it is my duty as I have already fully explained to you— if you think it is yours to obey the Spaniard, so to stop me, be it so: but be assured that the attempt will cost the lives of many brave men—this you may be sure of.'

Eventually, the chief let Pike and his men continue on their way. The soldiers set out, following the hoofprints of the Spaniards' horses along a path that would later become known as the Santa Fe Trail. They continued moving south to what is now Great Bend, Kansas, where they reached the Arkansas River.

Pike's party left the Pawnee village and headed south on what would later become the Santa Fe Trail.

There, Lieutenant Wilkinson took five privates and some native guides and left Pike in order to explore the lower Arkansas River. Wilkinson and his men paddled down the river in two canoes, floating to its junction with the Mississippi River. Thenhe headed north, back home to St. Louis. Although Wilkinson's trip was far shorter than Pike's, it was not easy. The journey took about two and a half months, and three of his men deserted along the way. Wilkinson, however became the first white American to travel through the region that would one day be known as Oklahoma.

On October 28, 1806, Pike and his remaining 16 men continued to follow the Spanish up the Arkansas River and into South Park, a tableland in the southern Rockies in Colorado. Here, they explored the area south of what is now Leadville, Colorado. As the days went by, Pike knew that he had to make a decision: Should he turn around or continue on his mission? Already, the party had encountered some snowy weather, and the men lacked warm winter clothing. But Pike chose to press on. "I determined to spend no pains to accomplish every object," he wrote, "even should it oblige me to spend another winter in the desert."

On November 15, Pike peered through his telescope to see a tall mountain that looked like a "small blue cloud." The party headed toward the peak. On

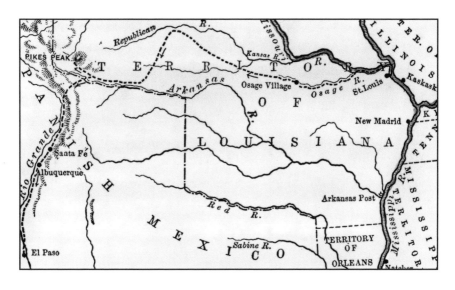

Pike's route through the West

November 23, he set up camp in southeastern Colorado, in what is now Pueblo. The site would serve as a base camp for Pike's men while he tried to climb the tall, snow-covered mountain he had seen looming in the distance. From the highest point in the region, Pike believed he might get a good look at the land around him.

On November 24, 1806, Pike, Robinson, and two other men set out toward the mountain. The big peak was more than 40 miles (64 km) away from the party's campsite, although it looked closer. Pike and his three companions spent several days hiking toward the mountain but only reached the big peak's foothills. From his vantage point on a smaller peak, Pike described the breathtaking view of the land around him. "The unbounded prairie was overhung with clouds, which appeared like the ocean in a storm; wave piled on wave and foaming, whilst the sky was perfectly clear where we were."

Pike estimated that the mountain he wanted to climb was still about 15 or 16 miles (24 or 25 km) away. To get there, he and his men would have to wade through deep snow and endure subzero temperatures and biting winds—all with little food and no winter clothing. Pike gave the order to turn around and return to camp. In his journal, Pike named the mountain Grand Peak. He was convinced it would never be scaled, or climbed. He wrote in his journal: "I believe that no human being could have ascended to its [peak]."

Pike was not the first person to see the mountain. Native people knew of the peak, the Spanish had seen it, and American trappers had been there. Later, another Army officer exploring the region would also catch a glimpse of the peak. In 1842, John Charles Frémont would record in his

> *Pikes Peak, also known as America's Mountain, is more than 14,100 feet (4,300 m) high. In 1820, four Americans, climbed to the top of Pikes Peak. During the California gold rush, the mountain became an important milestone on the trails to the West. The motto for many miners was "Pikes Peak or Bust!" And in 1893, Katharine Lee Bates was so impressed by her trip to the top of Pikes Peak that it inspired her to write the lyrics to the song "America the Beautiful."*

A view of Pikes Peak

journal that he had spotted "Pikes Peak." The name stuck, even though Pike never made it to the top.

After returning to camp on November 29, Pike and his cold, hungry men packed up and prepared to continue their expedition. The party marched for two days until they came to a fork in the Arkansas River. Pike was suddenly faced with an important decision: Which branch of the river should the group travel along? He and his men were in rough shape, so he chose to continue following the Spanish along Four Mile Creek. Unfortunately, the creek soon came to an end, and the men lost the trail of the Spanish. At that point, Pike's party turned inland toward the Rocky Mountains. On December 13, they reached the South Platte River.

The men spent a miserable Christmas huddled around a huge bonfire, trying to keep warm. By that time, many of them had been forced to cut up their blankets to replace their worn-out socks. At night, they attempted to get some rest on the hard, snowy ground. In his journal, Pike tried to make the best of their predicament. He wrote, "We spent the day as agreeably as could be expected from men in our situation."

On Pike's birthday, January 5, 1807, he received an unwelcome surprise. After following a river that they believed to be the Red, Pike was stunned to discover that they were, in fact, again on the Arkansas. He realized that he and his men had been traveling in a circle. They were back to where they had started a month before. In his journal, Pike wrote, "This was my [twenty-eighth] birth-day, and most fervently did I hope never to pass another so miserably." Pike probably would have been even more miserable if he had known his journey was only halfway over.

Pike knew he would have to enter the mountains

in search of the Red River. He left behind a private and the translator in a crude fort, along with some worn-out horses that were no longer useful.

Pike and his men approach the front range of the Rocky Mountains.

On January 14, he and his remaining men entered the Rockies. The worst part of the journey was just ahead. ✍

7 WINTER IN THE ROCKIES

Chapter

ഐഐ

Pike's party spent the next several weeks lost in the Rocky Mountains. The men pushed their way through waist-high snowdrifts. They were forced to camp out in the open, in weather so cold that few could sleep. Nine of the men soon got frostbite, including Pike's two best hunters. When Pike himself tried to shoot a buffalo for food, he found that his hands shook so badly he couldn't aim straight.

In his journal, Pike described the feeling of watching his dinner run away: "After crawling about one mile in the snow, got to shoot eight times among a gang of buffalo, and could plainly perceive two or three to be badly wounded ... to our great [horror] all were able to run off. By this time I had become extremely weak and faint, being the fourth

Stretching about 3,000 miles (4,828 km) across North America, the Rocky Mountains are the largest mountain range on the continent. The Rockies begin in Alaska, stretch down through Canada, and cut through the states of Montana, Idaho, Wyoming, Utah, and Colorado before ending in New Mexico.

day since we had received [food]." Pike later described how he was "attacked with a giddiness of the head, which lasted for some minutes."

Two more exhausted, frostbitten men were left behind in the camp to tough it out. Pike gave them what little meat was left and some ammunition. As their commanding officer, he did his best to encourage the two frightened men, but the situation looked grim. Pike said he "made use of every argument in my power to encourage them to have fortitude to resist their fate; and gave them assurance of my sending relief as soon as possible. We parted, but not without tears." Less than a week later, another man would be left behind to await rescue.

Of the 22 men who had begun the journey with Pike, only 11 now remained. The little party next turned south, crossing the Sangre de Cristo Mountains into present-day southern Colorado. On the other side of the mountains, Pike hoped to find warmer weather. On the third day in the range, however, the men marched through a snowstorm.

By then, some of Pike's soldiers had had enough.

One man, John Brown, told Pike that it was "more than human nature could bear, to march three days without sustenance through snows three feet deep, to carry burthens [burdens] only fit for horses." Soon after hearing Brown's complaint, Pike was finally able to kill a buffalo. After the men had eaten, Pike promised Brown that if he or any other man said anything like that again, they would be shot. He wrote later, "They all appeared very much affected."

On January 27, 1807, the men found a small stream that they believed would lead them to the Red River. They followed the stream, entering a sandy valley now known as Great Sand Dunes in southern Colorado. Eventually, the party did come to a big river. Although Pike thought it was the Red

Great Sand Dunes National Monument

River, he had actually reached a tributary of the Rio Grande. He was dangerously close to the Spanish.

By February 1807, Pike had wandered into Spanish territory. He crossed to the western side of the river he believed was the Red and began to build a fort. The little fort was quite crude. To get in, a person had to lie on his belly and crawl over a log that stretched across a moat. The men had filled the moat with water. After crossing, one was forced to crawl through a small hole under a wall.

After work on the fort had begun, Pike sent two relief parties back for the horses and men who had been left behind. Only one man came back with the relief parties. The other two were too sick to come.

Instead, they sent along pieces of their gangrene-ridden toes, begging Pike not to abandon them. He wrote, "Ah! little did they know my heart, if they could suspect me of conduct so ungenerous." The two men would later be rescued by Spanish troops.

Robinson, the young physician who was traveling with the party, decided it was time to take his leave of Pike. He needed to find his way to Santa Fe in order to collect a debt. Robinson followed Humboldt's inaccurate map and ended up getting lost. Luckily for him, he was captured by Ute Indians. His capture probably saved him from dying of starvation or freezing.

Robinson was captured by Ute Indians and taken to Taos, New Mexico.

The Ute first took Robinson to Taos, in present-day New Mexico, and then on to Santa Fe. There, Robinson lied to Spanish officials, telling them he had just separated from a party of hunters. But Mexican governor Joaquin del Real Alencaster was suspicious. He immediately sent out patrols to look for the so-called hunting party. ✑

8 A Prisoner of Spain

❧⟨✕⟩❧

Although Zebulon Pike would always insist that he believed he was camped on the Red River, some historians think that the explorer knew exactly where he was—and what he was doing. Pike may have wanted to be captured by the Spanish. Then he could scout out the best trails into Santa Fe. Once there, he would be able to take notes on the settlement's defenses and resources.

If Pike did indeed want to be taken captive by the Spanish, he soon got his wish. On February 26, Spanish troops discovered Pike and his men and arrested them. Some historians think that this is when his mission truly started. In his journals, Pike described the meeting with the Spaniards. "What," he said, when told he was on the Rio Grande,

Some historians believe Pike knew he was traveling on a tributary of the Rio Grande River.

The Palace of the Governors, where Pike was questioned by Spanish authorities, is the oldest surviving public building in the United States. The adobe structure was built in the early 1600s. In addition to being a home for the Spanish governor of New Mexico, the palace held the territorial legislature, courts, a library, a post office, and a jail. In 1909, responsibility of the building was turned over to the Museum of New Mexico, which established the building as a showcase of the state's history. In 1960, the palace was designated a registered National Historic Landmark.

"is not this the Red River?" He continued, "I immediately ordered my flag to be taken down and rolled up, feeling how sensibly I had committed myself in entering their territory, and conscious that they must have positive orders to take me in."

Pike was right. With armed Spanish soldiers escorting him, the officer and his party arrived in Santa Fe in early March. Pike was one of only a handful of Americans who had ever visited the territorial capital. As he and his men made their way through Santa Fe, excited residents crowded around them to get a good look.

And what a sight the Americans were! Instead of U.S. Army soldiers, Pike and his fellow explorers looked more like unsuccessful mountain men. Because their uniforms had worn out, the men were wearing clothing that they had stitched together out of animal skins. The men's boots had also become

useless, and they had wrapped their feet in rags. The soldiers were dirty, unshaven, and their long, greasy hair hung limply at their shoulders. Pike wrote, "This appearance was extremely mortifying to us all, especially as soldiers."

Pike was one of the few Americans who visited Santa Fe.

In Santa Fe, Pike was reunited with Robinson. And he was introduced to Governor Alencaster. While interviewing Pike at the Palace of the Governors, Alencaster got right to the point. "You come to reconnoiter our country, do you?" Pike

73

quickly and coolly replied, "I marched to reconnoiter our own."

But some historians believe the orders were written with the idea that they might indeed be read by the Spanish if Pike were captured.

For his part, Pike initially found the governor "haughty and unfriendly." Because of the roughness of his questioning, Pike thought that "war must have been declared" between Spain and the United States.

Alencaster, however, soon warmed up to Pike, calling him "a man of honor and a gentleman." He gave the American a new shirt and tie (made by his own sister back in Spain) to replace his filthy, old clothing. He also held a fancy dinner in honor of the American. Alencaster even allowed Pike's soldiers to keep their weapons as a "point of honor." Then he had Pike placed under military guard and marched down to Chihuahua, the capital of Mexico's northern territories, for questioning. In Chihuahua, Pike's papers could also be more accurately translated into Spanish.

Along the way, the Spanish treated Pike and his companions

Pike's papers from the 1806–1807 expedition were not released by the Mexicans until the early 1900s, after an American historian discovered them in Mexico's archives. They were finally published in 1908. Today, his party notes, letters, and maps are kept in the National Archives in Washington, D.C.

The Spanish questioned Pike at the Palace of the Governors in Santa Fe.

well. Pike became especially fond of one Spanish offi-cer, Lieutenant Facundo Melgares. He had commanded the troops that chased Pike across the Plains the year before. But now he and Pike became friends. Pike later wrote that the Spaniard treated him with "polite-ness and friendship." He came to think of Melgares as "my brother soldier."

On the 260-mile (418-km) trip from Santa Fe to Chihuahua, the men passed through present-day Albuquerque, New Mexico, and El Paso, Texas. The people along the way welcomed the strangers and held dances and barbecued food. Pike later remarked about their "heaven-like qualities of hospitality and kindness."

Pike was not just enjoying his sightseeing trip. During the journey to Chihuahua, and later back to the United States, the American officer took notes on scraps of paper. He recorded several important details about the Southwest and its geography. He

While in Spanish custody, Pike and his men were exposed to local residents' customs and foods.

also wrote down information about Spanish New Mexico. Pike knew that if his escorts caught him taking notes, they would confiscate them. He had a solution. "In the night I arose," Pike wrote. "I took small books and rolled them up in small rolls and tore a fine shirt to pieces and wrapped it round the papers and put them down the barrels of the guns ... the remainder we secured about our bodies under our shirts."

When Pike visited Santa Fe in 1807, he estimated the population to be about 4,500. Today, the city's population is closer to 62,000. Pike liked the people he met in New Mexico. He called them "the bravest and most hardy subjects in New Spain."

NORTH AMERICA

Scale.

100 200 300 400 500 600 700 800 900 1000 Miles.

9 A SUSPECTED SPY

❦

Upon reaching Chihuahua in April, Pike was greeted by General Nemesio Salcedo, commander of New Spain. Salcedo was not inclined to be friendly toward his American guest. "You have given us and yourself a great deal of trouble," he told the young lieutenant. Refusing to be bullied, Pike responded, "On my part entirely unsought, and on that of the Spanish government voluntary." This was Pike's way of letting the governor know that he hadn't intended to cause trouble and that he felt the actions of the Spanish had been quite unnecessary. Salcedo immediately demanded to see Pike's papers. The papers were again confiscated, but Pike was allowed to keep personal letters from Clara.

Despite the general's cool reception, Pike was

A map of North America from the 1800s showing the United States and Mexico warmly welcomed by the people of Chihuahua. During the day, Pike visited with people throughout the city or spent his time studying the Spanish language and writing letters and accounts of his journey. In the evening, he was treated to fancy dinners where singers serenaded him with songs in French, Italian, Spanish, and English.

Although Pike was treated well, the Spanish were determined to learn whether or not he was a spy. Upon arriving in Chihuahua, Pike was housed with Juan Pedro Walker, a New Orleans native who spoke Spanish, French, and English. After the United States had purchased the Louisiana Territory, Walker chose to move to Mexico and become a citizen of Spain. Walker greatly angered Pike during his stay by asking the American to pay rent while living in his home.

Pike immediately realized that Walker had been ordered to report every word he and his men said back to the Spanish. The lieutenant quickly used Salcedo's spy to his own advantage. "Robinson and myself frequently used to hold conversations in [Walker's] presence purposely to have them communicated," Pike wrote in his journal, "but he at last discovered our intentions, and told us, that if we calculated on making him a carrier of news, that we were mistaken; that he despised it." Salcedo had plenty of other spies around Chihuahua. Pike later

Pike (right) touring Spanish Mexico and discussing that region's boundaries

wrote, "In this city the proverb was literally true, that 'the walls had ears,' for there was scarcely any thing could pass that his excellency did not known in a few hours after."

During Pike's stay in Chihuahua, he continued

During his second trip, Pike purchased two baby grizzly bears from an Indian. Pike's men carried the small creatures in their laps, feeding them milk as they traveled. The pair became quite tame and followed the soldiers around like puppies. Before returning home, Pike made arrangements to have the bears sent to President Thomas Jefferson.

When the animals began to grow larger, Jefferson turned them over to Charles Willson Peale in Philadelphia. Although cute and friendly when they were small, the two bears became dangerous and aggressive as they grew older. They were eventually killed, stuffed, and displayed in Peale's Museum.

recording his observations. One of his notes discussed the terrible state of medicine in Mexico. On April 4, Pike recorded the following incident:

Visited the hospital, where were two officers, who were fine-looking men, and I was informed had been the gayest young men of the province. They were [wasting] away by disease, and there was not a physician in his Majesty's hospitals who was able to cure them; but after repeated attempts, all had given them up to perish. This shows the deplorable state of medical science in the provinces. I endeavored to get Robinson to undertake the cure of these poor fellows, but the jealousy and envy of the Spanish doctors made it impracticable.

For the most part, his time in Mexico was pleasant and uneventful. Unfortunately, Pike's refusal to keep his opinions to himself got him into some trouble. Toward the end of April, Salcedo sent a representative to Pike, asking him to

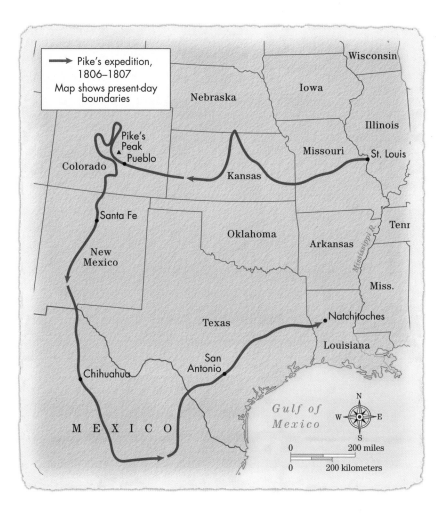

Pike's expedition, 1806–1807
Map shows present-day boundaries

Wisconsin

Iowa

Nebraska

Illinois

Missouri

St. Louis

Pike's Peak

Pueblo

Colorado

Kansas

Santa Fe

Oklahoma

Tenr

New Mexico

Arkansas

Miss.

Natchitoches

Texas

Louisiana

San Antonio

Chihuahua

Gulf of Mexico

M E X I C O

N
W — E
S

0   200 miles
0   200 kilometers

Pike's various expeditions took him into unexplored regions west of the Mississippi.

stop speaking about certain topics for the remainder of his visit. It seemed that the general feared Pike's opinions might lead to unrest and rebellion. Pike, however, refused. He told the representative, "I should always give my opinions freely, either as to politics or religion."

In the end, Salcedo decided it was more important

to keep the peace with the United States than to punish Pike for spying. Pike's death at the hands of the Spanish might set off a war between the two countries. Salcedo decided to let the Americans go free. Later, when writing a report to send to Spain, the general said he believed Pike was a spy. He also stated that Alencaster had made a serious mistake in sending Pike to him: The trip south had allowed Pike, an American Army officer, to collect valuable military information about Mexico for the United States. As a result of his decision to send Pike south, Alencaster was later removed from office.

In June 1807, Pike, Robinson, and six of the soldiers were escorted by Spanish troops through Texas and back to the United States. The Spanish had decided that the rest of the Americans would remain behind. All but one of the men were held in Mexico for two years before they were sent back home. One, however, had a much longer stay. During a drunken fight, Sergeant William Meek killed his friend, Private Theodore Miller. After a trial in New Spain, Meek was held as a prisoner in Mexico for 14 years.

Once Pike left New Spain, the Spanish sent an official letter of protest about his mission to Washington, D.C. The letter demanded that the United States apologize for sending a spy into its territory. Secretary of State James Madison refused to offer an apology, responding that Pike was an explorer, not a spy, and that his mission had never included espionage. As a result of the incident, the two nations broke off diplomatic relations.

On July 1, Pike and his party were escorted to Natchitoches in Louisiana. After a long, dangerous, and disappointing journey, the men couldn't have been happier. Pike wrote, "Language cannot express the gaiety of my heart when I once more beheld the standard [flag] of my country waved aloft."

James Madison refused to apologize to Spanish officials.

At home, Pike found both good news and bad news awaiting him. He learned he had been promoted to the rank of captain while he was away. And in New Orleans, he was reunited with Clara and their daughter. But Pike also learned of Wilkinson's treasonous plans, which had been discovered and made public. Worse still, this treachery had stained Pike's own reputation.

In an effort to redeem himself in the eyes of Jefferson and the United States, Wilkinson betrayed

Aaron Burr was accused of treason in 1807.

his old friend Aaron Burr. In the summer of 1807, during Burr's trial for treason, Wilkinson was the chief witness against him. Burr was found not guilty, however, and Wilkinson was branded as a traitor for the rest of his life. The foreman of Burr's jury, John Randolph, called the former general "the only man that I ever saw who was from the bark to the very core a villain."

Pike was dragged further into the messy affair when some of his letters were introduced as evidence during Burr's trial. Pike was attacked in newspapers across the nation, called by one editor a "parasite of Wilkinson" and the "beast of Santa Fe" by another.

Pike was furious. He asked Henry Dearborn, the U.S. secretary of war, for help in repairing his reputation. Dearborn agreed, telling people that Pike's expedition was useful and advantageous to the United States and all Americans.

From New Orleans, Pike and his family sailed to

New York. There, he was given a chilly reception by President Jefferson, who did not consider Pike an effective explorer. Jefferson probably felt this way because Pike had not recorded the same types of geographic and scientific information that Lewis and Clark had carefully collected on their journey into the West. The president may also have been suspicious of Pike's ties to Wilkinson and Burr. While the men on the Lewis and Clark mission had received extra pay and land as rewards for their service to the country, Pike and his men received neither. Later, when Pike tried to bill the U.S. government for surveying services, his bill was denied.

Pike believed that he didn't receive the honors he deserved because of his connection to Wilkinson. He was probably correct. Most historians today are convinced that Pike was innocent of treason and had no prior knowledge of Wilkinson's plan. They point to Pike's later service to his country as a sign of his patriotism. ❧

10 THE WAR OF 1812

Chapter

❦

After his second expedition, Pike settled back into the life of an Army officer. In 1809, he and his family moved to New Orleans, where Pike later served as a deputy quartermaster general. In the Army, a quartermaster general is in charge of providing food and clothing for the troops.

In 1810, Pike published *An Account of Expeditions to the Sources of the Mississippi and Through the Western Parts of Louisiana*. It included everything he could remember of his travels. At first, the book was not a success. With many grammar and spelling mistakes, Pike's account of his trip was difficult to understand. It also included few dates. Because of its poor initial sales, Pike's publisher went bankrupt after printing the book.

Pike and his family moved to New Orleans in 1809. The U.S. flag had been raised in that city six years earlier, following the Louisiana Purchase.

Although the book wasn't perfect, it was the first written account of the American Southwest and eventually became very popular. Thanks to Pike and his reports, people became more interested in settling in this part of the United States. With a copy of Pike's book in hand, many Americans packed up and headed west. In addition, American officials learned more than they had ever known about the political, military, and economic situation in Mexico and its territories. And traders and merchants saw the region as a new market for their goods. As a result of his book's rise in popularity with the public, Pike—by now a major in the Army—also became a celebrity.

Over the next few years, Pike and his family traveled from one military post to another. Pike served at Fort Bellefontaine in St. Louis and Fort McHenry in Maryland. He also served at several southern posts, including Natchez, Mississippi, and New Orleans, Louisiana.

In June 1812, the War of 1812 broke out between the United States and Great Britain. The United States entered the conflict to protect its foreign trade. It also wanted to end British impressment, in which American sailors were taken off American ships and forced to serve in the British navy. During the war, many battles took place in Canada, as the United States attempted to take Canadian land and end British influence in the Great Lakes region.

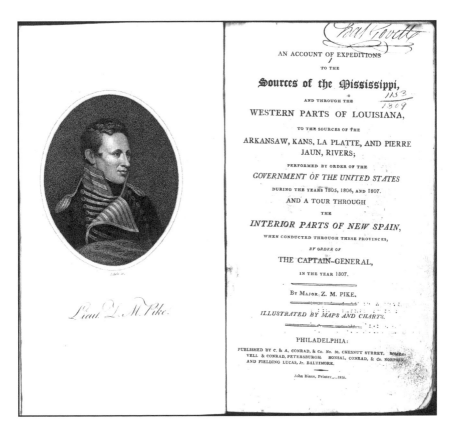

AN ACCOUNT OF EXPEDITIONS

TO THE

Sources of the Mississippi,

AND THROUGH THE

WESTERN PARTS OF LOUISIANA,

TO THE SOURCES OF THE

ARKANSAW, KANS, LA PLATTE, AND PIERRE
JAUN, RIVERS;

PERFORMED BY ORDER OF THE

GOVERNMENT OF THE UNITED STATES

DURING THE YEARS 1805, 1806, AND 1807.

AND A TOUR THROUGH

THE

INTERIOR PARTS OF NEW SPAIN,

WHEN CONDUCTED THROUGH THESE PROVINCES,

BY ORDER OF

THE CAPTAIN-GENERAL,

IN THE YEAR 1807.

BY MAJOR Z. M. PIKE.

ILLUSTRATED BY MAPS AND CHARTS.

PHILADELPHIA:

PUBLISHED BY C. & A. CONRAD, & Co. No. 30, CHESNUT STREET, SOMER-
VELL & CONRAD, PETERSBURGH. BONSAL, CONRAD, & Co. NORFOLK.
AND FIELDING LUCAS, Jr. BALTIMORE.

John Binns, Printer....1810.

Pike's book ultimately made him famous, but initial sales were poor.

At the beginning of the war, Pike was promoted to the rank of colonel. He soon learned that he would be sent to attack Montreal in Canada. Finally, he saw his chance to distinguish himself, clear his name, and prove his patriotism and bravery. In a letter to his father from New York, Pike wrote, "If we go into Canada, you will hear of my fame or of my death."

On April 27, 1813, Pike—now a brigadier general—commanded a force of 1,700 troops in an attack on York (now Toronto), the capital of Upper Canada. Henry Dearborn, Pike's superior officer and the former secretary of war who had defended Pike, was supposed to lead the attack, but he became ill. Pike and his men were ferried across Lake Ontario from Sackets Harbor in New York.

As Pike's troops advanced, the outnumbered British and their Indian allies fled. Outside the British fort, Pike conferred with his officers. Suddenly, an ear-splitting roar shook the ground beneath them. A British gunpowder magazine where ammunition was stored had been set off. Nearly 100 British and American soldiers were killed. Another 180 were wounded by the blast.

One of the wounded was General Pike. A flying rock hit him, tearing a huge hole in his back and gravely wounding him. His first thoughts, though, were for his men and the battle. He told his troops, "Push on my brave fellows and avenge your general."

Pike was carried off the battlefield and put onboard an American ship. He died a few hours later. According to some eyewitnesses, he perished with a smile on his face as he heard the sounds of the British in York surrendering. Pike was just 34 years old. His body was returned to Sackets Harbor and buried there. After Pike's death, his widow Clara moved back to Kentucky, where she died in 1847.

After Pike's death, former president Thomas

Pike's death onboard an American ship during the War of 1812

Jefferson responded in writing to a letter from Alexander von Humboldt. He had complained that Pike had stolen his map and report of Mexico and used it in his 1810 book without the scientist's permission. Jefferson's words seem to summarize Pike's life:

Pikes Peak serves as an ongoing reminder of the explorer's courageous expeditions.

Whatever [Pike] did was on a principle of enlarging knolege [sic] and not for filthy shillings and pence of which he made none from that book. ... Let me solicit [sic] your forgiveness then of a declared hero, of an honest and zealous patriot, who lived and died for his country.

Although Pike never achieved the level of fame and fortune he so eagerly sought, his adventures in the Southwest provided valuable information about that region and encouraged settlement there. While there was debate during his lifetime about whether he was an explorer or spy, patriot or traitor, Pike was undeniably courageous. Today, Pikes Peak in Colorado serves as a permanent reminder of his bold expeditions into unknown territory.

In 1846, more than three decades after her husband's death, Clara Pike was finally awarded $3,000 by the government for Pike's services.

PIKE'S LIFE

1793
Zebulon's father is sent to command Fort Washington, near Cincinnati, and brings his family with him

1779
Born in Lamberton, New Jersey

1790

1779
Jan Ingenhousz of the Netherlands discovers that plants release oxygen when exposed to sunlight

1789
The French Revolution begins with the storming of the Bastille prison in Paris

WORLD EVENTS

1799

Receives orders to take command as a second lieutenant; within eight months, he's promoted to first lieutenant

1794

Joins his father's company at the age of 15 as a cadet

1800

1795

J. F. Blumenbach writes his book *The Human Species* thus laying the foundation of anthropology

1799

The Rosetta stone, which was the key to understanding Egyptian hieroglyphics, is found near Rosetta, Egypt

PIKE'S LIFE

1801

Elopes with his
18-year-old cousin,
Clara Brown,
to Cincinnati

1802

Is transferred to a
new infantry unit in
Fort Knox, Kentucky

1801

Ultraviolet radiation
is discovered

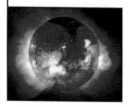

1802

United States Military
Academy founded
at West Point

WORLD EVENTS

1803

Is transferred
to a post in
Kaskaskia, Illinois;
Clara gives birth to a
daughter, Clarissa

1805

Is assigned to lead an
expedition to find the
source of the
Mississippi River and
leaves in August

1806

Is given new orders to
explore the western
mountains and to spy
on the Spanish; he
leaves in July; in
November, Pike
locates a tall
mountain in southern
Colorado and names
it Grand Peak

1805

1803

The Louisiana
Territory, which
essentially doubles
the size of the United
States, is purchased
from France

1805

General anesthesia is
first used in surgery

1806

Emperor Francis II
dissolves the Holy
Roman Empire, which
was founded in 800

PIKE'S LIFE

1807

Is captured by the Spanish in February; is released in June

1809

Serves as deputy quartermaster general in New Orleans

1810

Publishes *An Account of Expeditions to the Sources of the Mississippi and Through the Western Parts of Louisiana*

1810

1809

Louis Braille of France, inventor of a writing system for the blind, is born

1810

Bernardo O'Higgins leads Chile in its fight for independence from Spain

WORLD EVENTS

1812

Promoted to
rank of colonel

1813

Is wounded in a blast
and dies later during
the War of 1812

1815

1813

Jane Austin writes
Pride and Prejudice

1812

Napoleon's shattered
army leaves Russia;
Tchaikovsky's famous
"1812 Overture" is
later written about
this military campaign

DATE OF BIRTH: January 5, 1779

BIRTHPLACE: Lamberton, New Jersey

FATHER: Zebulon Pike (1751–1834)

MOTHER: Isabella Brown (1753–1809)

EDUCATION: Self-taught

SPOUSE: Clarissa Brown (1783–1847)

DATE OF MARRIAGE: 1801

CHILDREN: Clarissa (1803–1837); four others died in childhood

DATE OF DEATH: April 27, 1813

PLACE OF BURIAL: Sackets Harbor Military Cemetery, Jefferson County, New York

In the Library

Alter, Judy. *Exploring and Mapping the American West.* New York: Children's Press, 2001

Burgan, Michael. *The Louisiana Purchase.* Minneapolis: Compass Point Books, 2002.

Calvert, Patricia. *Zebulon Pike: Lost in the Rockies.* New York: Benchmark Books, 2003.

Stefoff, Rebecca. *The War of 1812.* New York: Benchmark Books, 2001.

Look for more Signature Lives books about this era:

James Beckwourth: *Mountaineer, Scout, and Pioneer*

Crazy Horse: *Sioux Warrior*

Geronimo: *Apache Warrior*

Sam Houston: *Texas Hero*

Bridget "Biddy" Mason: *From Slave to Businesswoman*

Sarah Winnemucca: *Scout, Activist, and Teacher*

Additional Resources

On the Web

For more information on *Zebulon Pike*, use FactHound to track down Web sites related to this book.

1. Go to *www.facthound.com*
2. Type in a search word related to this book or this book ID: 075650998X
3. Click on the *Fetch It* button.

FactHound will fetch the best Web sites for you.

Historic Sites

Fort Pike State Historic Site
27100 Chef Menteur Highway
New Orleans, LA 70129
504/662-5703
To visit the fort named after Zebulon Pike

Sackets Harbor Battlefield
State Historic Site
505 W. Washington St.
Sackets Harbor, NY 13685
315/646-3634
To visit a historic site where battles were waged during the War of 1812 and Zebulon Pike is buried.

broadswords
swords with wide, usually two-edged blades that are designed for slashing rather than thrusting

cartridges
containers that hold bullets or pellets and the explosive that fires them

espionage
the act of spying, or the work of a spy in trying to gain national or economic information that is of a secret nature

gangrene
death of soft tisssue when the blood supply has been cut off to that part of the body

haughty
very proud and prone to looking down on other people

infantry
the part of an army that fights on foot

patriots
people who love their country and are prepared to fight for it

scruples
strong feelings about what is right that prevent someone from doing wrong

tableland
a flat, elevated region; a plateau or mesa

tributaries
streams or rivers that flow into larger streams or rivers

tuberculosis
a highly contagious bacterial disease that usually affects the lungs

vantage point
a position that affords a broad, overall view of a place or situation

Source Notes

Chapter 1

Page 13, sidebar: Donald Jackson (Editor). *The Journals of Zebulon Montgomery Pike*, Volume 1. Norman, Okla.: University of Oklahoma Press, 1966, p. vii.

Chapter 2

Page 19, sidebar: Eugene W. Hollon. *The Lost Pathfinder: Zebulon Montgomery Pike*. Norman, Okla.: University of Oklahoma Press, 1949, p. 36.

Page 22, line 5: Ibid, p. 39.

Page 22, line 9: Ibid.

Chapter 3

Page 26, line 16: Merrill D. Peterson. *Thomas Jefferson and the New Nation*. London: Oxford University Press USA, 1975, p. 768.

Page 30, sidebar: Theodore Roosevelt. *The Winning of the West*, Volume 3. Lincoln, Neb.: University of Nebraska Press, 1995, p. 124.

Page 33, line 3: *The Journals of Zebulon Montgomery Pike, Volume 1*, p. xxiv.

Chapter 4

Page 38, line 8: Ibid, p. 48.

Page 38, line 14: Ibid.

Page 40, line 3: Ibid, p. 78.

Page 41, sidebar: Ibid, p. 126.

Page 41, line 20: Ibid, p. 87.

Chapter 5

Page 45, line 6: Stephen G. Hyslop. "An Explorer or a Spy?" American History, August 1, 2002, Vol. 37, Issue 3, p. 58.

Page 48, line 14: John Upton Terrill. *Zebulon Pike*. New York: Weybright and Talley, Inc., 1968, p. 85.

Page 50, sidebar: *The Journals of Zebulon Montgomery Pike, Volume 1*, p. 300.

Page 50, line 16: Ibid, p. 304.

Page 52, line 2: Donald Jackson (editor). *The Journals of Zebulon Montgomery Pike, Volume 2*. Norman, Okla.: University of Oklahoma Press, 1966, p. 27.

Page 52, line 17: Ibid, p. 28.

Chapter 6

Page 56, line 5: *The Journals of Zebulon Montgomery Pike, Volume 1*, p. 328.

Page 56, line 16: *The Journals of Zebulon Montgomery Pike, Volume 2*, p. 374.

Page 58, line 23: *The Journals of Zebulon Montgomery Pike, Volume 1*, p. 344.

Page 58, line 27: *Zebulon Pike*, p. 138.

Page 59, line 16: *The Journals of Zebulon Montgomery Pike, Volume 1*, p. 350.

Page 60, line 18: Ibid, p. 351.

Page 62, line 14: Ibid, p. 362.

Page 62, line 23: Ibid, p. 328.

Chapter 7

Page 65, line 10: Ibid, p. 369.

Page 66, line 3: Ibid, p. 370.

Page 66, line 14: Ibid.

Page 67, line 1: Ibid, p. 371.

Page 67, line 9: Ibid.

Page 69, line 5: Ibid, p. 381.

Chapter 8

Page 71, line 14: Ibid, p. 384.

Page 72, line 22: *Zebulon Pike*, p. 182.

Page 73, line 4: *The Journals of Zebulon Montgomery Pike, Volume 1*, p. 392.

Page 74, line 1: Ibid, p. 286.

Page 74, line 7: "An Explorer or a Spy?"

Page 74, line 12: *Zebulon Pike*, p. 190.

Page 75, line 5: "An Explorer or a Spy?"

Page 76, line 3:
http://www.nps.gov/jeff/LewisClark2/Circa1804/WestwardExpansion/Early
Explorers/ZebulonPike.htm

Page 77, line 5: *The Journals of Zebulon Montgomery Pike, Volume 1*, p. 424.

Page 77, sidebar: http://southwest.library.arizona.edu/hav1/body.1_div.7.html

Chapter 9

Page 79, line 4: "An Explorer or a Spy?"

Page 80, line 21: *The Journals of Zebulon Montgomery Pike, Volume 1*, p. 420.

Page 81, line 1: Ibid, p. 422.

Page 82, line 6: Ibid, p. 414.

Page 83: line 4: Ibid, p. 419.

Page 85, line 16: Ibid, p. 447.

Page 86, line 14: "An Explorer or a Spy?"

Page 86, line 21: Ibid.

Chapter 10

Page 91, line 7:
http://www.nps.gov/jeff/LewisClark2/Circa1804/WestwardExpansion/Early
Explorers/ZebulonPike.htm

Page 92, line 19: "An Explorer or a Spy?"

Page 94, line 1: *The Journals of Zebulon Montgomery Pike, Volume 2*,
pp. 387-388.

Farish, Thomas Edwin. *The History of Arizona*. San Francisco: The Filmer Brothers Electrotype Company, 1915

Hollon, Eugene W. *The Lost Pathfinder: Zebulon Montgomery Pike*. Norman, Okla.: University of Oklahoma Press, 1949

Hyslop, Stephen G. *"An Explorer or a Spy?" American History* 37: 3 (August 1, 2002)

Jackson, Donald (editor) *The Journals of Zebulon Montgomery Pike, Volumes 1 and 2*. Norman, Okla.: University of Oklahoma Press, 1966.

National Park Service. "Zebulon Pike: Hard-Luck Explorer or Successful Spy?" http://www.nps.gov/jeff/LewisClark2/Circa1804/WestwardExpansion/EarlyExplorers/ZebulonPike.htm

Peterson, Merrill D. *Thomas Jefferson and the New Nation*. London: Oxford University Press USA, 1975

Pike, Zebulon Montgomery. *An Account of Expeditions to the Sources of the Mississippi and Through the Western Parts of Louisiana*. Philadelphia: C & A Conrad, 1810. Located at http://www.artsci.wustl.edu/~landc/html/pike.html

Pike, Zebulon Montgomery. "Journal of a voyage to the source of the Mississippi in the years 1805 and 1806." Located at http://www.amphilsoc.org/library/mole/p/pike.htm

Roosevelt, Theodore. *The Winning of the West, Volume 3*. Lincoln, Neb.: University of Nebraska Press, 1995.

Terrell, John Upton. *Zebulon Pike: The Life and Times of an Adventurer*. New York: Weybright and Talley, Inc., 1968

Robin S. Doak has been writing for children for more than 16 years. A former editor of *Weekly Reader* and *U*S*Kids* magazine, Doak has authored fun and educational materials for kids of all ages. She is a past winner of the Educational Press Association of America Distinguished Achievement Award. She lives with her husband and three children in central Connecticut.

Image Credits

Minnesota Historical Society/John Casper Wild, cover (top), 4-5; Image courtesy of Capt. William D. Bowell Sr. Library, Artist Ken Fox, info@riverrides.com, cover (bottom), 2, 97 (top); MPI/Getty Images, 8, 81, 86, 91, 100 (top right); North Wind Picture Archives, 11, 17, 29, 31, 32, 34, 39, 47, 51, 59, 61, 64, 69, 73, 75, 76, 85, 99 (top right and bottom), 100 (top left); Library of Congress, 12, 96 (bottom right), 97 (bottom); Corbis, 14, 53, 57; The Granger Collection, New York, 18, 20, 22, 63, 93, 96 (top), 99 (top left), 101; Hulton Archive/Getty Images, 24; Francis G. Mayer/Corbis, 27; Historical Picture Archive/Corbis, 36, 44; Richard Hamilton Smith, 40; Bettmann/Corbis, 42, 54, 88; Mary Evans Picture Library, 49; Academy of Natural Sciences of Philadelphia/Corbis, 67; M. Dillon/Corbis, 68; Jay Syverson/Corbis, 70; Michael Maslan Historic Photographs/Corbis, 78; James L. Amos/Corbis, 94; Image Ideas, 96 (bottom left); Photodisc, 98, 100 (bottom).